THE DAY OF YAHWEH

PART OF A DISSERTATION SUBMITTED TO THE
FACULTY OF THE GRADUATE DIVINITY SCHOOL, IN
CANDIDACY FOR THE DEGREE OF DOCTOR OF
PHILOSOPHY

BY

JOHN M. P. SMITH

Published by Left of Brain Books

Copyright © 2021 Left of Brain Books

ISBN 978-1-396-31943-3

First Edition

All rights reserved. No part of this publication may be reproduced, distributed, or transmitted in any form or by any means, including photocopying, recording, or other electronic or mechanical methods, without the prior written permission of the publisher, except in the case of brief quotations embodied in critical reviews and certain other noncommercial uses permitted by copyright law. Left of Brain Books is a division of Left Of Brain Onboarding Pty Ltd.

THE DAY OF YAHWEH.

THE origin of the idea of the Day of Yahweh must be sought in the pre-prophetic stage of Israel's history. The first appearance of the conception in the Old Testament is in the prophecy of Amos, where it is clearly defined and formulated. The idea which Amos found already existing and occupying a large place in the thought of the people was apparently a conception of the day as a time when a period of great glory and prosperity was to be inaugurated for Israel. Naturally such a day was greatly desired. Whence came this idea? It seems to be a development of several ideas in combination. One of these is the conception of a divine mission which early took possession of the consciousness of Israel.[1] Tradition exhibits many traces of such a conception. The founders of the nation and all her great leaders are said to have had in mind a unique position for Israel among the nations. Utterances to this effect are common in the J and E documents,[2] and, belonging as they do to some of the earliest of Israel's historical records, it is not probable that they are wholly without basis in facts. They may, therefore, be properly taken as evidence for the existence in very early times of a hope for a glorious future of the nation as Yahweh's representative in the world.

In further support of the existence of some such ambition as this may be urged the presence of similar hopes among Semitic peoples in general.[3] The national character of Semitic gods seems best explained on the supposition that small and weak families, clans, and tribes submitted to the dominion of larger and more powerful communities because of some necessity, such as conquest, lack of food, or need of protection and assistance against powerful enemies. In such a union the superiority of the god of the more powerful body of people was acknowledged, and the god of the weaker people was reduced to subordinate rank. As this process continued, a nation gradually came into

---

[1] *Cf.* FRANTS BUHL, *American Journal of Theology,* Vol. II, p. 767.
[2] *E.g.,* Gen. 12:2 ff.; 18:18 ff.; 27:29; 28:14; Exod. 19:5 f.; 34:10; Numb. 23:9; 24:9, 17.
[3] W. R. SMITH, *The Religion of the Semites,* 2d ed., pp. 75-81.

existence, and the original tribal god developed into a national god.⁴ But the fact of his having reached this dignity did not rob him of his original expansive force; his nature remained essentially the same, and his ambition for power would carry him on to universal dominion, were his adherents sturdy and aggressive enough to attain that goal. It was therefore the natural and proper desire of every Semitic nation to extend the influence of its own particular god to the farthest possible limit. This could best be accomplished through the conquest of new territory over which the sway of the god might be established. Hence wars of conquest, which were at the same time religious wars, were of unceasing occurrence.

Assyrian records furnish the best illustrations of this spirit of expansion in political and religious affairs. The wars of Assyria were preeminently religious wars. Every king in every campaign declares himself to have been incited, emboldened, and prospered by his nation's gods. Kings felt and declared themselves to be the agents of the gods, and regarded it as one of their chief duties to widen the dominion of the gods and to manifest their power.⁵ Esarhaddon, for example, well expresses the animating spirit of Assyrian warfare thus: "The names of the great gods they invoked together and trusted to their power. I, however, trusted in Ashur, my lord, and like a bird out of the mountains I captured him and cut off his head. *In order to exhibit the might of Ashur, my lord, before the eyes of the peoples,* I hung the heads of Sanduarri and Abdimilkuti upon the necks of their great men."⁶ The inscriptions of Tiglath-pileser I., Shalmaneser II., Tiglath-pileser III., Sargon, Sennacherib, Esarhaddon, Ashurbanipal, and others are full of illustrations showing the place and influence of religious ideas in connection with the national territorial development.⁷ The evident desire was that Ashur should be acknowledged as the supreme deity throughout the known world. The kings certainly regarded him as such and commonly spoke of themselves as

---

⁴ So MENZIES, *History of Religion*, pp. 79 ff.; D'ALVIELLA, *Idea of God*, pp. 20 ff.; *et al.*

⁵ *Cf.* McCURDY, *History, Prophecy and the Monuments*, Vol. I, pp. 63 f.; SAYCE, *Early Israel and the Surrounding Nations*, pp. 248 f.

⁶ The Six-Sided Prism, *Cylinder A*, col. i, ll. 43 ff.

⁷ *Cf.* Sennacherib, *Taylor-Prism*, col. i, ll. 10 ff., 63; i, 42 f.; .iii, 42; iv, 43; Esarhaddon, *Cylinder A*, col. ii, l. 45; iii, 7-12, 40-48, 53; iv, 19-25, 38-47; Ashurbanipal, *Annals*, col. iv, l. 34; viii, 8 ff.; ix, 112 ff.; etc.

kings of the four quarters of the world over which Ashur had given them dominion.[8]

The amazingly rapid spread of the religion of Mohammed is another illustration of the efficient service rendered by religious ideals in the furtherance of political development. The religious and ethical principles upheld by Mohammed were certainly purer and more vigorous than those of the earlier Arabic religions opposed by him, and his success was, no doubt, largely due to this fact; but it seems probable that the old Semitic idea of a national god upon whose people there rested an obligation to extend his dominion had much to do in arousing the extraordinary zeal and energy with which the new religion was propagated, and that chiefly by force of arms. For such a religion and such a god success was the best recommendation; a recital of the triumphs already achieved was one of the best arguments for inducing still other peoples to acknowledge the supremacy of the new religion and the new god. Moreover, confidence engendered by successes already won carried the victors on to fresh contests and victories for their god.

In view of such corroborating testimony from without, it is not strange to find evidence within Israel of a similar laudable ambition for Yahweh and of a hope for the time when he would bring great glory to his people. That this hope originated at a very early date is evident, since it appears strongly in the earliest literature. Moreover, as suggested by Professor McCurdy,[9] the possession of such a hope is a necessary presupposition to any satisfactory explanation of the fact that Israel was able to obtain and hold for herself a home among the tribes of Canaan, poorly disciplined as she was and beset by foes on every side. Her strong faith in Yahweh's power and in his purpose to bring glory to himself through Israel gave her courage in the face of all sorts of dangers and difficulties. Hence it is that every forward step during the period of the conquest and the years immediately following seems to have been preceded and accompanied by a great revival of zeal for Yahweh. Furthermore, the course of Israel's early national history was not unfavorable to the growth

---

[8] For the same idea see the closing tablet of the Dibbara Legend, translated by JASTROW in *Religion of Babylonia and Assyria*, p. 535, and by W. MUSS-ARNOLT in R. F. HARPER'S *Assyrian and Babylonian Literature* ("The World's Great Books," Aldine edition; New York: D. Appleton, 1901), p. 314.

[9] *Op. cit.*, Vol. II, pp. 110 f.

of this idea of a glorious destiny. Beginning with Saul and continuing through the days of Solomon, victory and prosperity had come to Israel in no small measure. Even in later centuries the reign of David was looked back upon longingly as a sort of golden age, and ideals of the future were shaped in accordance with the glorified and magnified traditions of the Davidic days. Solomon extended his influence so far, established his kingdom so securely, and equipped himself so splendidly as to be the source of envy and wonder to all surrounding peoples. He was in a fair way to make Israel a world-empire such as Assyria and Babylon later came to be. After the check consequent upon the division of the kingdom, northern Israel, under the able leadership of the house of Omri, gradually reasserted herself. This new development was retarded by the long war with Syria, but by the time of Jeroboam II. Damascus was subdued, and Israel had attained prosperity and power second only to those enjoyed during the age of David and Solomon. History thus seemed to justify the popular hope of a gloriously bright future.[10]

In addition to this, the work of the earliest prophets tended in the same direction. All the prophets the time of Amos, with the possible exception of Elijah, seem to have foretold success and glory for their people.[11] They constantly emphasized the fact that Israel was Yahweh's people, and that, if Israel remained faithful to him, he would and must lead her on to victory.

Thus far we have found the hope of a great future for the nation through Yahweh's help to have been (1) fostered by tradition; (2) an outgrowth of the general Semitic conception of a God-given commission to enlarge the sphere of the divine authority; (3) a prerequisite as a source of inspiration and courage in the great work of the conquest of Canaan; (4) developed and strengthened by its apparent partial realization in the progress of the nation's history; and (5) enforced impressively upon the national consciousness by the nation's prophets, the spokesmen of Yahweh, the nation's God. In view of these facts the existence of such a conception of Israel's national destiny in the eighth century B.C. seems certain. It was not a conception of an exalted ethical and religious content, for ethical and religious standards were as yet comparatively low. It was rather the conception of a mission, one of the chief ends of which was to bring glory to those who fulfilled it.

---

[10] *Cf.* G. A. SMITH, *The Book of the Twelve Prophets*, Vol. I, pp. 49 f.
[11] *Cf.* 1 Kings 20:13, 28; 22: 6, 11, 12; 2 Kings 2:13-19; 13:14-19; 14:25.

A second and important element in the formation of the early idea of the Day of Yahweh was the conception of Yahweh which then prevailed.[12] The people were not far removed from polytheism, as is shown, among other things, by the frequency and ease with which in after years they took up with idolatrous rites; by the survival of the plural form אלהים; by the use of *teraphim;* by the incident of the calf-worship at Sinai; and by traces lingering in many words and customs.[13] The intermediate stage, monolatry, was essential as a stepping-stone to monotheism, and the religion of Israel in the eighth century was of this kind. Israel's God was only one among many gods; the name Yahweh as a proper name distinguished him from Chemosh, god of Moab, Milcom of Ammon, Baal of Phœnicia, and the gods of other surrounding peoples. This monolatrous worship persisted far into the prophetic period, monotheism not being fully accepted and established in the thought of the nation until the days of the exile.[14] The difference between Yahweh and other gods was but dimly realized in the early days of Yahwism. The points of resemblance between the worship of Israel and that of Canaan were more noticeable than the points of difference, and the constant endeavor of Israel's religious leaders was to keep the people from taking over so much of Baal-worship into the Yahweh-worship as to destroy the distinctive character of the latter. The preservation of true Yahweh-worship was essential to the development and continuance of national life and individuality. The Yahweh-religion was almost the only unifying influence which held together the heterogeneous and widely scattered elements of Israel. Yahweh's especial function was to be the deliverer of Israel in time of danger. He was emphatically a war-god, and it was as such that he was honored by Israel. He had proven his superiority to the gods of Egypt at the time of the exodus; and

---

[12] *Cf.* R. H. CHARLES, *A Critical History of the Doctrine of a Future Life in Israel in Judaism and in Christianity,* pp. 85 f.

[13] *Cf.* BAUDISSIN, *Studien zur semitischen Religionsgeschichte,* Heft I, pp. 55-65.

[14] See Judg. 6:31; 9:13; 11:24; Gen. 28:20 f.; Exod. 15:11; 18:11; 1 Sam. 26:19; 28:13; Amos 9:7; Ezek. 8:12; 9:9; etc. For a fuller treatment of the matter consult SMEND, *Lehrbuch der alttestamentlichen Religionsgeschichte* (2d ed.), pp. 193-200; MONTEFIORE, *Religion of the Ancient Hebrews* (="The Hibbert Lectures," 1892), pp. 228, 268 f.; McCURDY, *op. cit.,* Vol. III, pp. 370 f.; W. R. SMITH, *The Prophets of Israel* (new edition), pp. 59 ff.; SCHULTZ, *Old Testament Theology,* Vol. I, pp. 175 f.; BUDDE, *Religion of Israel to the Exile,* pp. 210 f.

again, in the attack upon Canaan, he had demonstrated his superiority to the Canaanitish Baalim by conquering them and their people. This was, indeed, the only kind of superiority that Israel was as yet prepared to appreciate. Her existence during the greater part of the pre-prophetic period was one constant struggle to maintain her place against the peoples of Canaan, and a god who could not, or would not, render efficient service in this contest was not likely to command her respect and adherence. The victories of Israel over her enemies were necessary, not only to her national existence, but also to her retention of the Yahweh-religion. The work of Elijah in his fearless opposition to Baal-worship, and the work of Elisha as the source of the inspiration, wisdom, and patriotism in the conduct of the war with Damascus which enabled Israel to achieve final victory, sealed Israel to Yahweh in closest allegiance.

Though the recognition and acceptance of Yahweh as Israel's God did not involve the denial of reality to the gods of neighboring peoples, but permitted them to be regarded as real deities holding relations with their worshipers similar to those existing between Yahweh and Israel, yet Yahweh was supreme in Israel and in everything relating to Israel, and thus, when the interests of Israel clashed with those of her neighbors, it was to be expected that he would bring about the triumph of his own nation. However, the recognition of the reality of the gods of the nations was a great hindrance to Israel's full realization of the true nature of her mission to the world. It shut off almost entirely the outflow of the altruistic spirit and left the conception of Israel's destiny to find embodiment in hopes for Israel's supremacy among the nations and Yahweh's dominion over the gods. It was a self-centered mission, a destiny founded on ambition for Israel, and jealousy for the honor of Yahweh.

Another source of light upon the origin of the idea of the Day of Yahweh is found in the political relations of early Israel with outside nations. After the fierce struggles connected with the early days of the settlement in Canaan, Israel seems to have adopted a policy of conciliation toward the Canaanites in whose land she was an unwelcome intruder. The battle led by Deborah and Barak was the last great conflict with the people of the land. Deadly enmity gave way little by little to peaceful intercourse. Conciliation was Israel's wisest course; dwelling in the midst of a numerous people far more advanced in civilization than herself, and ready to take advantage of any and every opportunity to drive her out of their territory, it was necessary for her to strengthen herself in every possible way. She therefore gladly admitted "strangers" into her ranks and threw open to them all the privileges of Israelites.[15] She gained much by accretions resulting from such a policy and by the friendly feeling thus cultivated toward neighboring tribes.

But, though Israel succeeded thus in bringing her immediate neighbors into harmony with herself, she was not suffered to develop her resources in peace. Her whole life up to the eighth century was one almost continual struggle for existence. Occupying, as she did, the most fertile oasis in northern Arabia, she was subjected to the onslaughts of less fortunate tribes who coveted the rich possession for themselves. Prior to David's time contests were waged with the Moabites, Ammonites, Amalekites, Philistines, Midianites, Edomites, and Syrians, deliverance being wrought for Israel under the leadership of Ehud, Shamgar, Gideon, Jephthah, Samson, and Saul. David's reign was a period of war and conquest resulting in great renown for Israel. The territory acquired by David began to revolt and slip away under Solomon's administration. The long struggle with Syria began in the reign of Baasha of Israel, and continued with bitter hostility down through the reigns of Jehoahaz and Jehoash. In addition to this there were skirmishes with the Philistines in the days of Nadab of Israel; war with Mesha, king of Moab, in the time of Jehoram; revolt and reconquest of Edom under Joash and Amaziah respectively. Moreover, Assyria appears upon the scene as collector of tribute from Jehu. The last great war, that with Damascus, was a long drawn-out agony for Israel; but at last Yahweh sent Israel a savior in the person of Assyria, and she enjoyed a brief respite from fighting. The feelings of an Israelite, as he looked back upon his nation's long struggle, can scarcely have been amicable toward those with whom he had waged so many conflicts. He rejoiced in the downfall of Damascus, and would have taken equal pleasure in the discomfiture of other hereditary foes. Revenge was a far sweeter thought to him than forgiveness, and one more likely to stir his enthusiasm and arouse his zeal.

The bearing of the preceding discussion upon the question of the origin of the idea of the Day of Yahweh may now be briefly summarized. The people of Israel in the eighth and ninth centuries had inherited and developed the idea

---

[15] For a discussion of the whole question of the place of "strangers" in Israel see BERTHOLET, *Die Stellung der Israeliten und der Juden zu den Fremden*, pp. 1-67.

that they were destined by Yahweh for great things. They thought themselves certain of attaining political preeminence. They were to be instrumental in demonstrating to the nations the superiority of Yahweh, Israel's God, over all the gods of the nations. With a conception of Yahweh as but one—howbeit the greatest one—among many gods, it was necessary for them to prove his greatness to the surrounding peoples who were in like manner proud of their own respective gods. Yahweh had repeatedly shown himself to be efficient and worthy of all confidence as a war-god. It was along this line that his superiority was to be proved to the nations. Yahweh had shown his pleasure in Israel and had manifested his power in recent days by overthrowing Damascus, her bitterest foe. How natural that the great majority in Israel should feel encouraged and should hope for the speedy coming of the day when Yahweh should manifest himself in behalf of his people and bring disaster and destruction to all their foes, thereby proving his own supremacy over all other gods and the superiority of his chosen people over all the peoples of other gods! The *popular* conception of the Day of Yahweh was, in short, that of a great day of battle on which Yahweh would place himself at the head of the armies of Israel and lead them on to overwhelming victory over all their enemies.[16]

---

[16] The view of HOFFMANN, *Zeitschrift für die alttestamentliche Wissenschaft* (=*ZATW*.), 1883, p. 112, that in the popular conception the Day of Yahweh was looked upon as a *feast* day has no support aside from the fact that the context of Amos 5:18 ff. takes up the question of feasts, and this is not sufficient to establish the usage in view of the indications favorable to the view adopted here. For other instances of יוֹם in the sense "day of battle" see Isa. 9:3 = יוֹם מִדְיָן, and Hos. 2:2 = יוֹם יִזְרְעֶאל; cf. Obad., vs. 11 = יוֹם אחיך, and Ps. 137:7 = יוֹם יְרוּשָׁלַםִ. The Arabic يَوْم is frequently used in the same sense; see the Qurân, Sura 45, vs. 13, where the expression "days of God" is interpreted by Arabic commentators as meaning days when God overthrows the infidels in battle. SCHULTENS, *Liber Jobi cum nova versione...et commentario perpetuo, etc.*, Vol. I, pp. 54 f., quotes in support of this usage the following passage from *Hamasa*:

من رأى يومنا ويوم بني التيم
اذا التف صبقه بدمه

"Who saw our day and the day of the sons of Teim,
When the dust was made coherent with its blood?"

In the hands of Amos this conception underwent a transformation. As heretofore it had been instrumental in stimulating the national spirit and life, so now, purified from its grosser elements, it is made to contribute to the development of the religious and moral life of the people. Instead of being the day of Israel's glorification at the expense of her enemies, it now became the day of her humiliation and chastisement at the hands of Yahweh. It was a complete reversal of all the hopes which Israel had so long centered in this day. The first announcement of the new doctrine (Amos 5:18 ff.) must have fallen upon the people with startling suddenness; it was a rude awakening from a pleasant dream.

The new conception of the day introduced by Amos was the outgrowth of the new idea of Yahweh which had taken possession of him. It was the practical application of his thought of God to the conditions of his age. For him Yahweh's predominant characteristic was righteousness (Amos 5:4-6, 24); and this called for a corresponding righteousness on the part of Israel. The peculiar relation she sustained to Yahweh only increased the obligation upon her to be righteous (Amos 3:2). In the presence of this demand for moral integrity Amos saw Israel's fearful depravity. Northern Israel had probably never before enjoyed such outward prosperity and political prestige as at this time.[17] Hints are not wanting in Amos of the great wealth and luxury of the times (Amos 3:10, 12, 15; 5:11; 6:4-8). But it was altogether too manifest that this was secured largely at the expense of the poor, and that cruelty and vice of every description abounded (Amos 2:6-8; 3:9, 10; 5:10-13). Even the women had sunk to the lowest depths of degradation (Amos 4:1-3), and the political leaders, as well as the religious leaders, were foremost in wickedness. Yet amid all this moral desolation, having no conception of Yahweh's demand for righteousness, the people prided themselves on the fact that Yahweh was with

---

and from *Omar ibn Keltsoum:* فما ابقت الايام ملمال عندنا "Nor have the days [*i. e.*, days of battle] left any resources in our possession." W. R. SMITH also (*Prophets of Israel,* Lecture III, note 15) refers to a section on the "Days of the Arabs" in the *Ikd* of Ibn Abd Rabbih, Egyptian ed., Vol. III, pp. 60 f., from which he cites the phrase "the days of Tamim against Bekr" (*Ikd,* p. 80) in illustration of the fact that among the Arabs the day of battle was often named after the combatants. See also the Arabic illustrations of the same usage cited by Gesenius in his commentary on Isa. 9:3, and by STEINGASS, *Arabic Dictionary, sub voce.*

[17] *Cf.* 2 Kings 14:25-28, and McCURDY, *op. cit.,* Vol. I, pp. 308 f.

them, and that evil therefore could not overtake them.[18] Realizing the righteousness of Yahweh and the wickedness of Israel as fully as he did, Amos was forced to the conclusion that nothing short of Israel's destruction would satisfy the demands of Yahweh's justice. As the instrument for the execution of Yahweh's judgment upon Israel, his attention was naturally turned to the invincible Assyrian army, whose victorious progress was ever drawing nearer and nearer to the borders of Israel. The nation was ripe for destruction; the destroying agent was close at hand; therefore the Day of Yahweh must be coming full soon—perhaps even in his own generation. It was to be the close of the existing degenerate age rather than the opening of a new and glorious one, as the people had fondly hoped.

With such a message Amos addressed northern Israel. Wellhausen has called attention to the artistic and dramatic way in which he introduced his startling announcement.[19] By denouncing the neighboring peoples and foretelling their destruction he raised the hopes of his listeners that the Day of Yahweh was about to come upon their foes, as they had long desired, only to dash those hopes to the ground with startling suddenness when he announced to them that judgment was about to fall upon them themselves. "Woe unto you that desire the Day of Yahweh," says Amos; "wherefore would ye have the Day of Yahweh? It is darkness and not light... Shall not the Day of Yahweh be darkness and not light, even very dark and no brightness in it?" This statement was followed up and reinforced by the declaration of Yahweh's hatred of their luxurious and superstitious worship, and his intention to drive Israel into exile because of her sins. In the face of incredulity, jeers,[20] and threats, Amos

---

[18] Amos 5:14 is suspected as a later insertion by Valeton, G. A. Smith, Volz, Nowack, Löhr, *et al.;* but in any case the blind confidence in the protecting presence of Yahweh which is there attributed to Israel was characteristic of her in the eighth century B.C.; *cf.* Mic. 3:11 and Judg. 6:13.

[19] *Die kleinen Propheten,* on Amos 2:14 ff.

[20] Amos 6:3. CHEYNE, *The Book of the Prophet Isaiah. A New English Translation,* p. 135 [=Polychrome Bible, or *SBOT*.], seems to regard this passage as testifying to the existence of two opposite views concerning the Day of Yahweh among the people in the time of Amos—the one looking forward to it eagerly as a time of joy for Israel, the other regarding it as an evil day, but supposing it to be still distant. If this was the case, all that Amos did was to adopt the darker view already existing and endeavor to convince Israel of its near approach. It seems more natural, however, to take this utterance of Amos as addressed to those who

persisted in his message. That day is to be ushered in by terrible portents in earth and heavens. Mourning and lamentation will take the place of the songs and feasts of the present. No one will be able to deliver himself from the universal calamity; all the workers of iniquity will perish. Not a ray of light illumines the darkness of the Day of Yahweh as described by Amos.[21] He saw that the popular idea of it as a time for Israel's glorification was deeply wrought into the life of the nation and was fraught with great danger to the higher interests of Israel, so that nothing less would do than to transform it completely and present it from an entirely new point of view. He must draw the thoughts the people away from illusive hopes and fix them upon stern realities.

In the formulation of his doctrine of the Day of Yahweh Amos did not break away completely from the past. He utilized some elements of the popular conception already existing, viz., the thought that Yahweh was to manifest judgment; that this would occur on a specific day; that this day would be a day of battle; that wonderful phenomena on earth and in the heavens would accompany the day; that in connection with the judgement punishment would fall upon the enemies of Israel and of Yahweh; and, above all, that it would be the time when Yahweh would vindicate himself in the sight of the whole world. But a radical departure from the popular idea is seen in the essential content of the new doctrine in accordance with which Yahweh's vindication involves Israel's discomfiture rather than her triumph. This was the necessary outcome of the new conception of Yahweh arrived at by Amos, for whom Yahweh's love of righteousness was greater and stronger

---

received his doctrine of the Day of Yahweh skeptically and ironically, blindly trusting in their present ease and security, and refusing to credit gloomy forebodings concerning a coming disaster of which they can see no signs. *Cf.* the interpretations of this passage given by Wellhausen, Gunning, Mitchell, Driver, and G. A. Smith.

[21] The promise of Amos 9:8b-15 is from a later hand. The argument against these verses is set forth in detail by VOLZ, *Die vorexilische Jahweprophetie und der Messias*, pp. 22-4; *cf.* G. A. SMITH, *op. cit.*, Vol. I, pp. 190-95. Among many others who assign them to a later time may be cited Wellhausen, Stade, Smend, Cheyne, Cornill, Marti, Nowack, Löhr, SCHWALLY, *ZATW.*, 1890, pp. 226 f.; PREUSCHEN, *ZATW.*, 1895, pp. 24-7; TORREY, *Journal of Biblical Literature*, Vol. XV, pp. 153 f.; J. TAYLOR, article "Amos" in HASTINGS' *Dictionary of the Bible*. For a defense of the authenticity of the passage see DRIVER, *Joel and Amos*, pp. 219-23.

than his love for his people. The effect of the application of this new idea of God to the doctrine of the Day of Yahweh was to lift the doctrine to a far higher plane and to make it subserve ethical and religious ends no less efficiently than it had thus far subserved the purpose of national and political development. The doctrine henceforth becomes one of the most powerful arguments of the prophets in their appeals to the people of Yahweh to forsake evil and cleave to that which is good.

Following the lead of Amos, the prophets continued to use the idea of the Day of Yahweh as a factor in the work of developing a purer national life and a keener moral sense. The pre-exilic prophets, however, with the exception of Zephaniah, did not give the idea a prominent place in their teaching. The term "Day of Yahweh" appears neither in Hosea, Micah, Nahum, Habakkuk, nor Jeremiah, and but a few times in the genuine utterances of Isaiah,[22] while Amos himself mentioned it only for the purpose of combating the erroneous popular conception in regard to it and of putting an entirely different meaning into it. This avoidance of the use of the term was due, perhaps, to a desire to refrain from calling to the remembrance of the people the perverted idea which it represented, an idea so strongly intrenched in the minds of the people that expulsion by direct attack seemed inadvisable; hence the earlier prophets chose the more indirect and effectual method of teaching correct fundamental ideas about Yahweh, the acceptance of which would drive out false conceptions of the Day of Yahweh.

Though the immediate successors of Amos avoided the use of the term for the most part, yet its content as formulated by Amos was taken up by them and strenuously enforced upon the nation. No important contribution was made to the idea by Hosea, Micah, or Isaiah; they adopted the view of Amos without essential change. The day of Yahweh's visitation continued to be thought of as a time for the punishment of Israel's sins.[23] Isaiah's doctrine of

---

[22] Isa. 2:12 ff.; *cf.* 5:18 f.; 7:18 ff.; 9:8– 10:4; 17:4 ff.; 22:5 ff.; chap. 13 and 34:8 are of later origin; see the commentaries of Duhm, Marti, and Cheyne on Isaiah.

[23] The passages in the books named after these prophets which present pictures of a bright future in connection with the coming of the Day of Yahweh are regarded by an increasing number of scholars as of late origin. See, *e.g.,* VOLZ, *Die vorexilische Jahweprophetie und der Messias;* NOWACK, *Die kleinen Propheten;* WELLHAUSEN, *Die kleinen Propheten;* W. R. HARPER, *American Journal of Semitic Languages and Literatures,* Vol. XVII, pp. 1-15; STADE, *ZATW.,* Vol. I, pp. 161-72; CORNILL, *Einleitung in das Alte Testament;*

the Remnant, however, opened the way for the announcements of a blessed future from later prophets. Nahum's vision is confined to a picture of the overthrow of Assyria; it is a rehabilitation of the popular conception of the Day of Yahweh, with a change in the reason assigned for the destruction of Israel's foes; it is no longer merely because they are foes to Israel and Israel's God, but because they are *wicked*.[24] This view was stated still more fully and forcibly by Habakkuk at a somewhat later date.[25] In the words of Professor Charles: "According to the primitive view, Yahweh was bound to intervene on behalf of his people on the ground of the supposed *natural* affinities existing between them, whereas, according to the view of Nahum and Habakkuk, his intervention must follow on the ground of *ethical* affinities; for Israel and the gentiles are related to each other as the righteous, צדיק, and the wicked, רשע (Hab. 1:4, 13)."[26]

The prophecy of Zephaniah was concerned with the Day of Yahweh as no previous one had been; it is the dominant thought everywhere present in his utterances. His conception agrees with that of Amos in that it supposes the day to be close at hand (1:7, 14), and to be a day of gloom and terror bringing judgment (1:2-6, 15 ff.), which is to fall primarily upon Yahweh's people, but also upon their enemies (1:7-18; 2:4-15). But Zephaniah goes farther than any of his predecessors, if we may suppose 3:8 to have come from him, in that he makes the judgment well-nigh world-wide. It is not, however, strictly speaking, a universal judgment, since certain "guests" are evidently excepted (1:7), and, furthermore, all are clearly not on the same level before Yahweh, for Judah is still regarded as Yahweh's people, and given blessings and

---

CHEYNE, *Introduction to tile Book of Isaiah,* and *SBOT.*, Part 10; DUHM, *Das Buch Jesaia* ("Handkommentar z. Alt. Test."); MARTI, *Das Buch Jesaia* ("Kurzer Hand-Commentar z. Alt. Test."), and article "Hosea" in *Encyclopædia Biblica;* HACKMANN, *Die Zukunftserwartung des Jesaia.*

[24] Chap. 1:1– 2:3 is assigned to a later date by Bickell, Gunkel, Cornill, Nowack, *et al.*, chiefly on the basis of its form and structure. However, all agree that this opening section gives a description of the Day of Yahweh fully in keeping with the spirit and contents of the rest of the book.

[25] Chap. 3 is quite generally regarded as a later addition; so, *e.g.*, Kuenen, Cheyne, Cornill, Wellhausen, Nowack, Driver, A. B. Davidson, G. A. Smith.

[26] *A Critical History of the Doctrine of a Future Life,* p. 94.

privileges at the expense of her enemies.[27] Out of this wide-reaching judgment a remnant of poor and afflicted people who trust in Yahweh's name, do no evil, and refrain from deceit is to remain and continue the relation between Judah and Yahweh.[28]

Jeremiah's work furnishes a good illustration of the prophets' dependence upon history. After his first utterances, which seem, like the words of Zephaniah, to have been called forth in connection with the Scythian invasion, little or nothing was heard from him until about the time of the battle of Carchemish, where Nebuchadrezzar appeared as the coming conqueror of western Asia. Jeremiah at once grasped the significance of this event and sounded the alarm for his people, continuing to preach repentance as the only way of escape from complete overthrow until the day his words were fulfilled. He did not call this coming calamity the Day of Yahweh, as Amos had done on a similar occasion in northern Israel, and as Zephaniah had already done in Judah. In the present state of the criticism of the book of Jeremiah it is difficult to determine just what the exact teaching of Jeremiah on this subject was.[29] But it seems to have included a simple, yet scathing

---

[27] PROFESSOR CHARLES' treatment (*op. cit.,* p. 98) of Zephaniah's teaching concerning the Day of Yahweh is based largely on the doubtful passages 2:8-10 and 3: 8-10. Moreover, the treatment is inconsistent in that part of its conclusions is based upon the authenticity of these verses, while part is based upon the supposition of their being interpolated.

[28] Zeph. 3:14-20 is considered late by most interpreters, *e.g.,* Oort, Stade, Kuenen, Schwally, Wellhausen, Budde, Cornill, Nowack, G. A. Smith. 2:8-11 is regarded as late by Oort, Wellhausen, Schwally, Budde, Nowack, G. A. Smith. Wellhausen and Schwally reject 3:8-10, and Budde, Nowack, G. A. Smith, 3:9, 10.

[29] All messianic passages are referred to a later time by VOLZ, *Die vorexilische Jahweprophetie und der Messias,* pp. 68-80. SCHWALLY, *ZATW.,* Vol. VIII, pp. 177-217, denies chaps. 46-51, and much of chap. 25, to Jeremiah. CORNILL, *SBOT.,* Part II, assigns to later times: 10:2-16; 17:19-27; 19:1– 20:6; chaps. 26-28, 34, 36-44, and 50-52, and many glosses besides. To these sections he adds, in his recently published pamphlet, *Die metrischen Stucke des Buches Jeremia reconstruirt* (Leipzig, 1901, pp. xiii + 43), the following passages: chap. 30; 31:1, 6-9a, 10-14, 21a, 38-40. GIESEBRECHT (*Handkommentar zum Alten Testament*) allows to Jeremiah only 1:1–17:18; chap. 18; 20:7-18; chaps. 22-24; 25:3 ff., 15-26; chap. 27; 32:6-17a, 24-44; chap. 35; much of the remainder he attributes to Baruch. NATH. SCHMIDT, article "Jeremiah" in *Encyclopædia Biblica,* regards as genuine only chap. 1; 2:2-13, 20-37; 3:1-5; 4:19 ff.; 7:3–9: 21; 10:19-21, 23-25; chap. 13(?); 15:5-9; 16:2-13; 18:1-17; 19:1 f., 10 f., 20:1-6; 21:1-10; 22:2-5, 10-19, 24-27; 23:9 ff., chaps. 24; 28; 32: 14

arraignment of Israel's wickedness and a call to immediate repentance. He lays greater emphasis than any of his predecessors upon the religious life as distinguished from the ethical. The sins he rebukes are idolatry, sun-worship, human sacrifice, a superstitious multiplication of sacrifices and offerings to Yahweh in the hope of thereby securing his favor, a blind trust in the inviolability of Jerusalem with its temple, and failure to keep the covenant and ordinances of Yahweh; see, *e.g.,* 7:4-10; 11:13; 15:4. He soon saw that Judah had gone too far in her downward path to be able to return, and that destruction was therefore inevitable. He looked upon Nebuchadrezzar as Yahweh's servant (27:6 ff.), through whom he was about to bring Judah and all the nations to judgment (25:15-26). He makes a great advance in that he admits the enemies of Judah to a Share in Yahweh's mercy; those who repent and learn Yahweh's ways will be restored to their own lands after their punishment; only the nations that refuse to obey Yahweh will be completely destroyed (12:14-17). However, the judgment is still national rather than individual in character; Jeremiah seems to have only introduced the thought of individualism into the religion of Yahweh and to have left the full working out of the idea to his successors.

The eschatological, apocalyptic tone of Zephaniah's threats of woe is almost entirely lacking in Jeremiah's preaching. He knows of no personal appearance of Yahweh upon earth, no extraordinary departure from the laws of nature, no threats of sudden visitation. His thought of Yahweh's activity and personality seems more spiritual than that of earlier prophets, and his presentation of the future is more sane and rational.

The pre-exilic conception of the Day of Yahweh was preeminently that of a day of judgment—a gloomy, forbidding event, fraught with punishment for

---

f.; chap. 34; 37:1-10, 11 ff. DUHM, whose commentary on Jeremiah (*Kurzer Handcommentar zum Alten Testament,* 1901) has just come to hand, assigns the following portions, with the exception of minor glosses, to Jeremiah, viz.: chaps. 2-6; 8; 9:1-21; 10:19-22; 11:15-20; 12:7-12; 13:15-17; 14:2-10, 17 f.; chap. 15; 16:5-7; 17:1-4, 9 f., 14-17; 18:13-20; 20:7-18; chap. 22; 23:9-15; 30:12-15; 31:2-6, 15-22; 38:22. To Baruch he assigns: 7:18; chap. 26; 27:2 f.; chap. 28; 29:1, 3-7, 11-15, 21-29; 32:6-15; 34:1-11; 35:1-11; 36:1-26, 32; 37:5, 12-18, 20 f.; 38:1, 3-22, 24-28; 39:3, 14a; 40:6—42: 9; 42: 13a, 14, 19-21; 43:1-7; 44:15-19, 24 f., 28*b;* chap. 45. The remainder of the book was added by various hands at various times, the messianic utterances and the oracles against foreign nations being among the latest additions. These latter come from as late a time as the end of the second century B.C.

Israel. The character of the times and the spirit of the people made it necessary for the prophets to take this view of the day whenever they touched upon the subject of Israel's future. They felt themselves to be reformers sent to a "wicked and adulterous generation," and they devoted all their energies to the work of arousing the people from their moral stupor and convincing them of their awful condition and of the near approach of punishment. To this end they uttered the threats of chastisement and painted the scenes of disaster so often associated with the thought of the Day of Yahweh. In a low stage of religious development messages of doom are often the most effective means of reaching men's minds and hearts. Mohammed's preaching was largely made up of this sort of material, and even Christian preachers have found it useful. Not that the early prophets deliberately employed this method of arousing the national conscience, though the form of expression is no doubt often embellished by rhetorical device intensified by oratorical fervor. They were giving expression rather to heartfelt convictions forced upon them by observation of social and political conditions and illuminated by the spirit of Yahweh. They strove earnestly to convince the nation of the truth of their message. Sometimes, as in the case of Zephaniah, they turned their attention to Israel's neighbors and proclaimed their destruction, perhaps with a not unnatural feeling of satisfaction; but primarily their preaching against the nations seems to have been for the purpose of warning Israel and calling her attention to the need of reformation, if she would avoid a similar fate. Nahum alone of the pre-exilic prophets reverts to the original pre-prophetic conception of the Day of Yahweh, and even though he does base his exultation over Assyria's approaching downfall upon ethical rather than natural grounds,[30] we cannot but feel that he stands on a lower moral plane than his predecessors and contemporaries in the prophetic office.

It was not till Israel was already feeling the bonds of captivity that Jeremiah changed his tone and began preaching words of encouragement and hope to Israel. Then he cheered her with promises of return from captivity and of restoration to her former glory. In this return and blessing northern Israel was also to have a share. A new covenant of love was to be established between Yahweh and his people, a covenant engraved upon their hearts; and the nation

---

[30] *Cf.* CHARLES, *op. cit.*, p. 94.

was to become a source of wonder to surrounding peoples because of her prosperity (33:9).

In thus painting the future of Israel bright, Jeremiah was followed by practically all succeeding prophets. The fall of Jerusalem and the exile of the people marked an epoch in religious as well as political history. As long as Jerusalem remained standing, the old superstitious belief in its charmed life continued, and prevented the people from coming to a true understanding of the relation existing between Yahweh and themselves. Hence both Jeremiah and Ezekiel had constantly reiterated the announcement of the coming destruction, and had thus prepared the people to understand, in some measure at least, the significance of the shock when it came upon them. The great disaster completely dissipated all false confidence, and opened the way for the propagation of new and grander conceptions of Yahweh and his will.

In connection with many other new teachings, the thought of Israel's restoration to Yahweh's favor was emphasized by both Jeremiah and Ezekiel, and this thought served to keep the disheartened people from deserting Yahweh and allying themselves with the successful gods of Babylon or lapsing into indifference, skepticism, and practical atheism. The Day of Yahweh is given a larger place in Ezekiel's thought than in that of Jeremiah, and this is natural in view of the fact that Jeremiah sought to reform the nation, and so to avert the impending disaster, while Ezekiel, especially after 586 B.C., concerned himself chiefly with the future of his people. Ezekiel conceives of the Day of Yahweh throughout as a day of battle quite in harmony with the pre-prophetic representation; but prior to 586 B.C. it is a day of battle on which Yahweh inflicts terrible punishment on Israel because of her sins (7:9 ff.; 13:5); after that date it becomes a day of battle on which Yahweh triumphs gloriously over the heathen world (30:2 ff.; 34:12; 39:8 ff.). The visitation of Yahweh upon Israel for the purpose of her purification is historically mediated, the Babylonians being the agents of Yahweh, just as the Assyrians had been thought of by Amos and Isaiah, and the Scythians by Zephaniah. The judgment upon Israel is also a national one as heretofore, but there is at least a suggestion (11:17-21; 21:25) of the idea of a judgment day for the individual, an outcome of Ezekiel's belief in the individual responsibility of each soul before Yahweh. The result of the chastisement of Israel will be her purification from sin and her loving allegiance to Yahweh, who will restore both branches of the nation to their homes and unite them under the rule of the messianic king. In connection with and preparatory to the deliverance of Israel, judgment is to fall upon the nations hostile to Yahweh, and especially upon Egypt (chaps. 30-32), the latter being singled out, no doubt, because of the prominent part she had played in bringing about Israel's calamity.

After restored Israel is established in the favor of Yahweh, the great final Day of Yahweh is to come upon the heathen world (chaps. 38, 39). The description of this day has in it apocalyptic elements, and is also conceived in a spirit of particularism, two things developed to their full extent in later Judaism. The forces of the heathen world are represented as gathering upon the mountains of Israel for the great battle against her. Under the leadership of Gog, prince of the land of Magog, the hosts assemble from all quarters till they seem like a storm, like a cloud covering the land. But they are permitted to assemble by Yahweh only that he may destroy them. Without any effort on the part of Israel they are to be annihilated. Violent earthquakes will overwhelm them with terror; in their confusion they will set upon and slay one another; pestilence will smite them, and Yahweh will rain fire, hail, and brimstone upon them. By this will all peoples be made to know Yahweh, Israel's Holy One. All that Israel has to do is to go forth and clean up the land after the conflict; seven months will it take them to bury the slain and seven years to burn their weapons, so great will be the slaughter.

In so far as Ezekiel's Day of Yahweh has to do with the nations, there is little advance beyond the original pre-prophetic idea. It is altogether a time of destruction for them, and that because they have presumed to regard lightly Israel and Israel's God. There is not a promise made to them, nor a hope of any description held out to them. Everything is done for the sake of Israel and Yahweh. This is a natural result of the harsh treatment that Israel received in her exilic experience, and is the point of view occupied by all the prophets of this period. Ezekiel evidently gives up the old idea of *one* day, and seems to have in mind rather an extended period of time. There are at least three definite and distinct stages in his "day," viz.: (1) a day upon Israel when Jerusalem falls; (2) a day upon Egypt and the nations when Israel is restored; and (3) a final day upon the representatives of the whole heathen world. The beginning of the formation of the dogma of the Day of Yahweh is manifested here in the absence of historical agents as mediators of the judgment upon Gog and his host, and in the universal character of the judgment inflicted upon Gog. In all previous judgment scenes the nations made to suffer the wrath of Yahweh have been those who have in various ways brought upon themselves the wrath of Israel, and they have been distinctly cited by name. But here the statement is broad and indefinite; it is a judgment upon the representatives of the non Israelitish world as such.

Not a prophet from the time of Ezekiel on through to the close of the activity of the prophets failed to show marked interest in things pertaining to the Day of Yahweh and the future which it was to usher in. Sometimes they used the terrors of the day as a scourge with which to whip the nation into line with their own lofty ideals of morality and religion; but more frequently they used it as a source of consolation and hope for the people in the midst of their discouragement and misery, presenting it in vivid colors as a time when Israel was to enter gladly upon the enjoyment of a glorious future.

In Ezekiel the day is noteworthy chiefly for the fact that the prophet conceives of it as the time when Yahweh will take vengeance upon his foes. The thought of vengeance was sweet to Israel during and after her bitter experience as a captive in a strange land. The true prophets were through every experience unswerving in their loyalty to Yahweh, and they believed, in later times at least, that his dominion was to be extended over the whole earth. But they had not yet succeeded in emancipating Yahweh from bondage to the people of his choice. Yahweh's supremacy over the world was only to be brought about in connection with the political exaltation of Israel, his own peculiar people, in triumph and power over all her enemies. They must be overthrown before Israel could attain the place necessary for her as Yahweh's representative in the earth.

A similar spirit to that prevalent in Ezekiel is exhibited in Isa. 13:2—14:23.[31] The Day of Yahweh here is preeminently, if not exclusively, a time when Yahweh's fury is to be poured out upon Babylon. The nations will gather against her, and the Medes especially will be stirred up against her—a pitiless

---

[31] This passage is assigned to the close of the exile by Duhm; CHEYNE, *Introduction*, pp. 67-78; G. A. Smith, Skinner, Marti, *et al.* The ode in 14:4*b*-22 is claimed for Isaiah by WINCKLER, *Altorientalische Forschungen*, Vol. I, pp. 193 f.; so also W. H. COBB, *Journal of Biblical Literature*, 1896, pp. 18-35; for a criticism of this position see CHEYNE, *Journal of Biblical Literature*, 1897, pp. 131-5.

and terrible people that cannot be turned from its purpose by the most lavish bribery. Babylon will be utterly destroyed, with all the horrors and barbarities of oriental warfare. The approach of this awful day, which is near at hand, will be signalized by an eclipse of the sun, moon, and stars, and by a great earthquake, shaking both earth and sky, and spreading terror everywhere. As a result of it, Judah will be restored to her own land, and the very peoples who have hitherto scorned and oppressed her will escort her home with honors and henceforth yield themselves as her servants. The old relation of taunter and taunted will be reversed; Israel will now make sport of fallen Babylon.

Isa. 42:13-17 is another picture of the Day of Yahweh which comes from this period. The manifestation of Yahweh will be in wrath against the nations, but will result for Israel in deliverance from captivity and return home under the guidance of Yahweh.

The same tone predominates in the prophecy of Obadiah, which belongs to the period of the exile.[32] The Day of Yahweh is "near upon all the nations," and Edom in particular is to receive just punishment for her unfeeling conduct toward Israel in her day of trouble. The destruction of Edom is to be accomplished, as in Isa. 11:14, by the united people of Israel. As Edom formerly oppressed Israel, so will Israel now oppress her, even to the point of annihilation. While Edom is thus blotted out of existence, the holy people left in Zion will take possession of Edom, Philistia, Ephraim, Samaria, Gilead, as far north as Zarephath, and of the cities of the south. Over all this Yahweh will reign as king.

Amos 9:8b-15, which exhibits a similar sentiment toward Edom, may belong to this period.[33] It gives great prominence to a description of the abundant material prosperity which Israel is to enjoy as the favored one of Yahweh in the era inaugurated upon his great Day.

The future of Edom and that of Israel are presented in striking contrast in Isa., chaps. 34 and 35, prophecies which seem to reflect the experiences of the latter part of the exile.[34] The Day of Yahweh is described as about to come

---

[32] For a defense of the exilic origin of Obadiah see G. A. SMITH, *The Book of the Twelve Prophets,* Vol. II, pp. 167-72.

[33] See footnote 21.

[34] These chapters are assigned to the later days of the exile by Dillmann, DRIVER, *Introduction,* 6th ed., p. 226, and Giesebrecht. G. A. Smith and Skinner place them after the

upon all the nations, and especially upon Edom, bringing fearful slaughter. As usual, it is to be accompanied by wonderful and terrible signs in earth and sky. The very soil of Edom is to suffer, and by its barrenness and desolation serve as a memorial of the great day; given over to thorns, thistles, wild beasts, satyrs, and the Lilith, it will be deserted of men and consumed by unending fire. But ransomed Israel will return to Zion; all her afflicted will be made whole; flowers and streams will unite to make the homeward journey pleasant; and every difficulty and danger will be removed from the way.

The hard experiences of the exile, and especially the attitude of the Edomites, seem to have given rise in this period to a spirit of bitter hatred of the nations, such as had never before existed. There is a feeling that Yahweh must vindicate his honor and his righteousness in the sight of the nations, but it seems at times as though this were over-shadowed in the mind of the prophet by a desire for revenge and retaliation upon the foes of Israel. Yahweh had so long been thought of as inseparably connected with Israel and her interests that even now in spite of the adoption of a monotheistic conception of God, it seems that the vindication of Yahweh can be only through a terrible judgment upon Israel's foes and an exaltation of Israel to a position of power and superiority over the nations.

The idea of the universality of the character of Yahweh, who was acknowledged in Israel, in consequence of her exilic experiences, as the only God of all mankind, bore fruit but slowly in the thought of the people. One result of the adoption of this larger conception of God was a gradual change in the thought of the Day of Yahweh. The necessity of Israel's vindication in the eyes of the world was by no means lost sight of, but alongside of and instead of the feeling of bitterness which had reveled in a contemplation of the destruction of outside nations there grew up a feeling of satisfaction in the thought of a possible conversion of the nations to Yahweh through the agency of Israel, his messenger to the world.

In Haggai and Zech., chaps. 1-8, no very definite statements are made concerning judgment upon the nations. Express mention of the Day of Yahweh is made by neither prophet. Echoes of it are heard in Hag. 2:6 f., 20-

---

beginning of the exile, but do not venture upon an exact date. Cheyne assigns them to the years 450-430 B.C., while Duhm and Marti put them at some time in the second century, but before the subjugation of the Edomites by John Hyrcanus in 128 B.C.

22, and Zech. 2:9, which passages are apparently reflections of the disturbed state of the Persian empire caused by the revolts against Darius. There is but scanty reference, moreover, to a work of preliminary purification in Israel to be performed by Yahweh before the full tide of prosperity can turn toward her (Zech. 3:9 and chap. 5). In the main, Israel's future is one to be desired rather than feared; she has already received her judgment and expiated her sins through the sufferings of the captivity. The only further judgment that may be expected is that upon the nations, and little attention is given to this; for the prophets are chiefly interested in the effort to restore the temple and thereby to arouse hope in Israel for the future. The effect of the judgment upon the nations will be, as usual, the exaltation of Israel in the eyes of the world. Instead of the little company of inhabitants now in Jerusalem, an overflowing population will be found therein. Yahweh himself will dwell there, and "City of Truth" will it be named. Yahweh's people will be gathered home from all lands to enjoy the rich fruitage of their own land as blessed by Yahweh. Best of all, so glorious will Israel become that many nations will seek Yahweh and join themselves to him in that day (Zech. 8:20-23).

The view of the future given in Isa. 2:2-4, *cf.* Mic. 4:1-4, is quite in keeping with that seen in Haggai and Zechariah. It contemplates a submission of the nations to the dominion of Yahweh, an exaltation of Jerusalem and its people in the sight of the world, Jerusalem as the center of the world's worship and the source of all instruction, and the inauguration of an era of peace. These ideas fit this period well and make it probable that this prophecy belongs here.[35]

The high hopes kindled by Haggai and Zechariah were not at once realized. After the completion of the temple, things went on practically as they had before; there was no wonderful manifestation of Yahweh's power on behalf of Israel; crops were no better; outsiders were no less scornful and malicious; Israel was apparently no nearer the attainment of her ideal. As a result of the reaction

---

[35] So Hackmann and Marti. A post-exilic origin is favored also by STADE, *ZATW.*, Vol. I, pp. 165 ff.; IV, p. 292; Wellhausen, Mitchell, CORNIILL, *Einl.*, pp. 137 f., 182; Volz, Cheyne, Nowack, *et al.* Duhm maintains Isaiah's authorship; so also BERTHOLET, *Die Stellung der Israeliten und der Juden zu den Fremden*, pp. 97 ff. RYSSEL, *Untersuchungen über die Textgestalt und die Echtheit des Buches Micha*, pp. 218-24, makes it originate with Micah. G. A. Smith maintains the possibility of its origin in the eighth century or in the beginning of the seventh. The view held by Hitzig, Ewald, Kuenen, De Goeje, *et al.*, that it is an older prophecy incorporated into both Isaiah and Micah, is now generally abandoned.

caused by this state of affairs, Israel sank deeper and deeper into despair. Even those hitherto most faithful now began to doubt Yahweh and to question whether after all it was worth while to worship him. To this disappointed and discouraged people the words of Malachi were addressed. They were aimed especially at three classes: (1) those who had become skeptical, doubting Yahweh's love for Israel and his righteousness; (2) the corrupt priesthood; (3) those who had contracted foreign marriages. A worldly spirit possessed all classes, and the fear of Yahweh was not in their hearts.

These facts determine the nature of the conception of the Day of Yahweh in Malachi. It is a day of judgment upon the wicked in Israel. No word of condemnation is spoken against the heathen. In fact, the book boldly asserts that the nations are truer worshipers of Yahweh than is Israel herself. The Day of Yahweh is upon Israel only, and its preliminary work now, as always, is one of purification. But such is Yahweh's love for Israel that he will send his messenger, even the great Elijah, before the great and terrible day, to warn the wicked of approaching destruction and save them from the wrath to come. No historical agent appears here as executor of the divine purpose, but, as in Ezekiel's representation of the overthrow of Gog, Yahweh himself does the work of destruction. The idea of a day of battle upon which Yahweh overthrows the enemies of himself and of his people for the sake of his own honor is here lost sight of; the judge and the culprit are the only parties considered; there are no spectators. The prophet does not go so far as to put gentiles on an equal footing with Israelites and to make righteousness, irrespective of nationality, the only requisite for divine favor, but leaves the gentiles completely out of consideration. Yahweh's Day is not only a time for the destruction of the wicked, but also the opening of a glorious age for the righteous. But the prophecy of Malachi does not dwell upon this phase of the day; the apparent aim of the book is to bring about a reform in worship and in other practical affairs, and the dark and terrible side of the Day of Yahweh is presented with the purpose of causing a halt in the wicked career of Israel.

From the time of Ezra on, a new environment was created for prophecy— an environment in which prophecy, in its real sense, could not live. The adoption of the written law as the rule and standard of life left little scope for prophetic activity. Everything was controlled by the legal and priestly spirit; the prophets themselves were priests at heart. The whole tendency of the priestly system was toward exclusiveness, and consequently the Jews withdrew themselves more and more from association and fellowship with outsiders, especially in religious matters. The Samaritan schism, with its accompanying rivalry and animosity, also tended to embitter the Jews against their neighbors.

To this period, perhaps, belong such utterances as those in Isa. 61:2; 63:1-6; 65:1—66:24.[36] Here the spirit of revenge appears at its worst. The remnant of Israel is promised all the blessings within the gift of Yahweh, while his enemies are to suffer every affliction and to perish by fire and sword. Those of them who escape will go to distant nations that have not heard of Yahweh and tell them of his deeds. Then will all the nations join in escorting Israel's exiles back and in rendering worship to Yahweh at the stated times in Jerusalem.

Some time after Ezra, Joel prophesied amid a scene of desolation and sorrow.[37] Swarms of locusts had devoured the fruits of the land; all food and drink were cut off; drought had combined with the locusts to render destruction complete. Even the regular offerings of the temple could no longer be kept up, and this was the climax of calamity in Joel's thought. He looked upon all this as an announcement of the approaching Day of Yahweh (1:15). In view of this he issued a call for a general day of fasting in Israel, and exhorted all to humble themselves in penitence before Yahweh and appeal to his mercy, in order that the destructive scourge might be removed and the terrible Day of Yahweh withdrawn. The expectation of pardon is grounded in the thought that Yahweh's honor in the sight of the world forbids him to destroy his own people utterly (2:17).

The day of fasting seems to have been observed and to have had the desired effect, for there follows immediately a description of returning prosperity, with promises of abundance in the coming days (2:18-27). After the realization of material blessings of every kind, the spirit of prophecy is to be

---

[36] So Duhm, Cheyne, Skinner, and Marti.

[37] The post-exilic origin of Joel is granted by most recent interpreters; *e.g.,* Wildeboer, Nowack, G. A. Smith, *et al.* place it in the second Persian century. DRIVER, *Joel and Amos* (*cf.* article "Joel" in *Encyclopædia Biblica*), puts it about 500 B.C., or possibly in the century after Malachi. Wellhausen makes it a late post-exilic work; *cf.* HOLZINGER, *ZATW.,* Vol. IX, pp. 89-131. For a recent defense of the early date see G. G. CAMERON, article "Joel" in HASTINGS' *Dictionary of the Bible.*

imparted by Yahweh to the whole nation, regardless of age, rank, or sex. The Day of Yahweh, which was an occasion of dread when near at hand, can be looked forward to at a distance as a joyful day—a dreadful day still, but for Israel's enemies, not for Israel. All who depend upon Yahweh will escape in that day. The scattered exiles of Judah will be gathered from all places whither they have been driven, and will be restored to Mount Zion. All the nations—among which Tyre, Sidon, Philistia, and Edom are especially mentioned—are to be summoned together for war in the "valley of Jehoshaphat," in the "valley of decision." There, in truly apocalyptic fashion, will they be annihilated by Yahweh because of their "violence done to the children of Judah." But Judah is to abide forever, and Jerusalem from generation to generation; she shall be holy, and strangers shall no more walk her streets. This world-judgment is apparently aimed by Joel at the peoples that have roused the enmity of the Jews in their mutual intercourse. The words "all nations" evidently cannot be taken literally, for the men of Sheba are still to survive (3:8).

Joel's Day of Yahweh was no longer a danger actually threatening the nation; as a result of the beginning made by Ezekiel and the further development, especially in Malachi, it was now a well-established *dogma*. No specific sins of the people of Israel are cited as occasioning the approaching calamity, and the offense of the gentile world is merely that of being hostile to Judah. No historical agent is used in carrying out the will of Yahweh upon the nations; he himself accomplishes their end by awful catastrophes in the natural world. Judah alone is to escape the terrors of that day, and her deliverance is due, not to her moral character, but to the fact that she acknowledges the sovereignty of Yahweh. The whole conception is eschatological and apocalyptic rather than prophetic, and it is dominated by the most intense particularism.

The same general apocalyptic style and spirit are characteristic of Zech., chaps. 9-14, which section probably comes from the troublous times of the Greek period, when the successors of Alexander were struggling among themselves for the possession of Syria, and the Jews were suffering the consequences of the strife.[38] The feeling which exists toward outside peoples

---

[38] In support of this date see especially STADE'S epoch-making articles in *ZATW.*, Vols. I, pp. 1-96; II, pp. 151-72, 275-309; and R. ECKARDT in *ZATW.*, Vol. XIII, pp. 76-109. *Cf.* also KUIPER, *Zacharia IX-XIV, Eene exegetisch-critische Studie* (1894); DRIVER,

is the same as that in Joel; the same enemies are threatened with woes, viz., Syria, Phœnicia, Philistia, and Egypt, with the addition of Greece, in a prominent way, natural in the later times. There is the same need of an initial work of purification in Israel as was demanded by Joel at first. But the punishment of Jerusalem that the Day of Yahweh will bring is, indeed, drastic; all nations will gather against her and capture her, subjecting her to the horrors of pillage and destroying half her population. But their triumph will be short-lived, for Yahweh himself will interpose with a terrible plague and will set them to slaying one another. As in Joel, Yahweh personally destroys the opponents of Israel, and adds to the awfulness of the occasion by working wonders in earth and sky.

After this inaugural work of destruction, a time of blessing opens up for Israel. However, a period of mourning is predicted for her, during which her people will weep for their former rebellion against Yahweh. This is a new thought in connection with the Day of Yahweh, and is not at all fully or clearly set forth; it is too general and indefinite to admit of accurate exposition. All idolatry is to be abolished and—what sounds strange, indeed—prophecy will cease to exist. Whereas Joel's ideal was that all of Yahweh's people might be prophets, this anonymous dreamer regards them as quite out of harmony with the blessedness and holiness of the days to come. He holds prophecy and deception to be practically synonymous terms—a sad commentary on the prophecy of his day. The dispersed Jews will be reassembled from all corners of the earth and brought back to Judah and Jerusalem. The earth will yield

---

Introduction, 6th ed., pp. 346 ff.; WILDEBOER, *Die Litteratur des Alten Testaments*, pp. 354 ff.; CORNILL, *Einleitung in das Alte Testament*, pp. 193-200; NOWACK, *Die kleinen Propheten*, pp. 346-54; G. A. SMITH, *The Book of the Twelve Prophets*, Vol. II, pp. 449-62. STAERK, *Untersuchungen über die Komposition und Abfassungszeit von Zech.* 9-14, agrees with Stade in the main, but dates 11:4-17 and 13:7-9 from the year 170 B.C. KUENEN, *Einleitung in das Alte Testament*, Vol. II, pp.386 ff., takes the position that chaps. 9-11 and 13:7-9 are made up of old fragments from the eighth century which have been worked over, supplemented, and arranged in their present form by a post-exilic editor, while 12:1–13:6 and chap. 14 originated about 400 B.C. WELLHAUSEN, *Kleine Propheten*, and ZEYDNER, *Theologische Studien*, Vol. XII, pp. 73 ff.; assign chaps. 9-14 all to the Maccabæan period; so also RUBINKAM, *The Second Part of the Book of Zecharia*, with the exception of 9:1-10, which he assigns to the time of Alexander. For a recent defense of the unity of the entire book see G. L. ROBINSON, "The Prophecies of Zechariah," in the *American journal of Semitic Languages and Literatures*, Vol. XII, pp. 1-92.

abundantly, and there will be no more curse upon it. Yahweh will be universally acknowledged as Lord and King, and Jerusalem, his dwelling-place, will be the gathering point of all nations; for everyone surviving from the slaughter of the nations will go up thither annually to keep the Feast of Booths. This is the most striking feature of the priestly character of this apocalypse, which is even more marked than that of Joel. Over all in Jerusalem will reign the messianic king who shall speak peace to the nations and have dominion over all the earth.

Zech., chaps. 9-14, does not present a coherent picture of the Day of Yahweh. It consists of a series of abrupt and fragmentary sketches of special features of that day, which are not easily brought together into a harmonious view. The same general ideals prevail as in Joel, but the particularism is not quite so intense, for, after being severely punished to bring them to their senses, the nations are given a part in the worship of Yahweh, though evidently not on an equal footing with the inhabitants of Jerusalem, while Joel has no place for them after their great overthrow on the Day of Yahweh. Zech., chaps. 9-14, does not make use of the term "Day of Yahweh;" all its views of the future are introduced by "in that day;" but that he has in mind the well-known Day of Yahweh is evident from 14:1, "A day is coming for Yahweh, etc." The idea seems, however, not to be limited to a single day, but to embrace a period of indefinite duration.

Two sections from the book of Isaiah seem to belong somewhere in the latter part of the post-exilic age, viz., chaps. 24-27 and 19:16-25.[39] The former is thoroughly in sympathy with Zech., chaps. 9-14, in almost every respect. The writer lives in a time of trial and suffering, but "in that day" all this will be done away. The nations will then receive their deserts; Judah will be saved, her exiles restored to her, and her reproach taken away in the eyes of all the world. Jerusalem will be the center of worship. In this apocalypse the universalistic element is less emphasized than in Zech., chaps. 9-14, there being only one reference to the nations as destined to enjoy the blessings of Yahweh (25:6 ff.).

---

[39] Isa., chaps. 24-27, can scarcely be definitely assigned with certainty. Ewald, Delitzsch, Dillmann, Kirkpatrick, Driver, *et al.* put it in the early post-exilic period. Kuenen, Cornill, SMEND (*ZATW.*, Vol. IV, pp. 161 ff.), Wildeboer, Cheyne, *et al.* assign it to the second Persian century. Duhm, Marti, *et al.* date it about 128 B.C. Chap. 19:16-25 is dated about 160 B.C. by Duhm and Marti, while Cheyne and Kittel assign it to the years 323-285 B.C.

In Isa. 19:16-25, while there is the usual prediction of woe upon the nations as they are represented in Egypt, it is, nevertheless, distinctly stated that this is only of a disciplinary nature, and that in consequence Egypt will repent and turn to Yahweh. Then follows the most generous and universal teaching in all prophecy. Egypt and Assyria—the apocalyptic name for Syria—representing the whole heathen world, are to share equally with Israel in the worship and service of Yahweh and in the enjoyment of his favor. "Blessed be Egypt, my people, and Assyria, the work of my hands, and Israel, mine inheritance." Not one advantage is assigned to Judah or Jerusalem. It is not even necessary to come up to Jerusalem to worship, for there will be an altar in the midst of Egypt. There will be constant intercourse between Egypt and Syria, and the two peoples will worship Yahweh together oblivious of all past enmity.

The book of Daniel, while it does not make reference to the Day of Yahweh by name, is nevertheless a gathering up of the fruitage of that idea. It is rather a record and an embodiment of the influence of the idea than the representative of any further change or development in the idea itself. It conceives of the Jews as occupying the position of supremacy in the world of the future, and of God's kingdom as finally overthrowing all others. The sinfulness of the nation and her unceasing opposition to God are alone responsible for her present trials and misfortunes. When chastisement has done its work of purification, God will deliver his people by his own power and exalt them above all peoples. Not only those living at the time of this consummation will be partakers of its glory, but the righteous Jews of former ages will arise from their graves and share in the happiness of these days. This thought of the resurrection, found also in Isa. 26:19, is rather an individual than a national conception such as the Day of Yahweh was, and its origin and development are to be connected with the growth of the idea of individualism as taught by Jeremiah and Ezekiel, rather than with that of the Day of Yahweh. But it is a national conception and supplements the thought of the Day of Yahweh in so far as it is due to a desire to add to the numbers and influence of the people of Israel in the time of glory upon which they are about to enter.

Through all the development of the idea of the Day of Yahweh in the Old Testament there clung to it certain characteristic features, some of which passed on into the later form of the idea found in the New Testament. They were never all equally prominent at one time, but received different degrees of emphasis according as the circumstances of the times and the thought of the nation changed. The very existence of the idea itself was a constant testimony to the fact that the nation felt its inability to work out its own destiny and trusted to Yahweh to complete the task. The ideal of its destiny changed much as the centuries passed, but the consciousness of the need of divine aid in attaining to this ideal grew ever more vivid and the activity of Yahweh in connection with it ever more prominent. There was also a recognition of the fact that the present age was only temporary, and must give way to a better and more glorious one which should abide forever. To inaugurate and establish this new era it was necessary that Yahweh himself should come to earth in person and institute the new order of things. This idea of the coming of Yahweh was very crude and anthropomorphic in the first stages of the idea of the Day of Yahweh, but as the thought concerning God became truer and more exalted, the coming of Yahweh was gradually thought of in a more and more spiritual sense. Connected with this coming of Yahweh was constantly pictured a series of great catastrophes in the natural world; marvelous portents on land and sea, in air and sky. These convulsions and shocks were just as numerous and conspicuous at the end of the development of the idea as at its beginning—indeed, rather more so after the Day of Yahweh began to take on apocalyptic coloring. This idea of wonders and horrors in the natural world accompanying a revolution in the moral and spiritual world was a natural outcome of the Hebrew conception of the physical universe, which took no account of universal and inviolable natural laws, but thought of Yahweh as directing the movements of the physical world in the most direct and personal way; it was his ordinary custom to punish religious backslidings by withholding the products of the soil. Nature, religion, and morals were directly and closely related to each other through Yahweh, and nothing was more natural than that a great change in the latter sphere should be introduced and accompanied by momentous actions in the former Sphere.[40]

The coming of Yahweh was always thought of as being for punitive purposes. Sometimes emphasis was laid upon the guilt of the nations as being the occasion of the punishment, sometimes on that of Israel. Usually both came in for a share of the chastisement, though upon one than the other; but

---

[40] *Cf.* STADE, *Geschichte des Volkes Israel*, Vol. II, pp. 225 f.

at times, carried away by indignation with his own people, the prophet lets the nations go unpunished, as in the case of Malachi; at other times the prophet's bitterness of feeling against the nations is so great that he exhausts himself in uttering denunciations and threats against them, letting Israel go free; such is the case with Nahum and several of the exilic prophets. But in any case the chief end of the day was accomplished in the revelation it made to the whole world of the holiness, majesty, and might of Yahweh, Israel's God. The time of the coming of the day was always left indefinite, though for the most part it was conceived of as near at hand, at most distant only a few years. But definite and specific predictions were not common with the prophets in any of their work, and they followed the prophetic custom with reference to this subject, leaving it in a state of indefiniteness that could not but add to the terrors which they so generously and vividly described—there was no telling when this awful visitation might fall upon the earth! Until the very latest days this coming was always conceived of as connected with some great historical movement of the times. Assyrians, Scythians, Babylonians, Persians, and Greeks were each in succession, as they appeared on the stage of world-history, heralded by the prophets as Yahweh's agents and instruments in administering the punishments of his great day. It is not till the incoming of apocalyptic prophecy with Malachi and Joel that these historical agents are ever dispensed with, but thereafter Yahweh is represented as personally executing his own decrees.

The last common characteristic of importance is the fact that the Day of Yahweh was always represented as introducing a new *political* state. The prophets were also patriots; they were no less loyal to Judah than to Yahweh; patriotism and religion were inseparably blended in them. Thus, even after the most universal type of monotheism had taken hold of the prophetic consciousness, they were wholly unable to think of Israel in the new kingdom of God otherwise than as the acknowledged head of the nations of the world. Jerusalem is to become the religious capital of the world, the abode of Yahweh, Israel's God, whither all the peoples shall come to do him homage. From a position of the slightest political significance in the world, Jerusalem and Judah are to be exalted to the place of greatest renown. The Day of Yahweh was always preeminently a vindication, in one way or another, of Israel, Yahweh's own people.

It appears as a result of this study that the development of the idea of the Day of Yahweh in Israelitish history was marked, not so much by the addition from time to time of new features, as by the expansion and deepening of elements already present, at least in germ, at the time of the origin of the prophetic conception. The great growth of the idea of God out of which the Day of Yahweh grew and with which it was ever vitally connected, necessarily affected the teaching of the Day tremendously. So likewise did the great change that manifested itself in reference to Israel's conception of her destiny as the people of Yahweh, as that conception changed gradually from one of political supremacy to one of religious and moral preeminence.

But the instrument of all this change both in constituent elements and in the idea as a whole—that which under divine guidance forced Israel's prophets and people to enlarge and enrich their conception of the Day of Yahweh—was the historical experience through which the nation was compelled to pass. No single prophetic conception better illustrates the prophet's relation to the history of his times than does this idea. It reflects clearly from generation to generation the political and social environment of the nation, adapting its form and content at all times to the demands of the historical situation, of which the prophets were always the best interpreters.

VITA.

I, JOHN M. P. SMITH, was born on the twenty-eighth day of December, 1866, in London, England. I prepared for college in the Light House Academy at Leominster, Herefordshire, and The Plantation House Academy at Dawlish, Devonshire. Removing, in 1882, to the United States, I later entered Des Moines College, whence I received the degree of A.B. in 1893. The next two years were occupied in teaching Greek and Latin in The Cedar Valley Seminary, Osage, Iowa. In the summer quarter of 1894 I entered the University of Chicago and began the study of theology; after a year's absence, spent in teaching, I returned to the University in the summer quarter of 1895, and remained in residence altogether fifteen quarters, giving especial attention to Old Testament language and literature, and to Assyrian. I received an appointment as Fellow in the Department of Semitic Languages and Literatures for the years 1897-98, 1898-99.

In pursuance of my Semitic studies I attended lectures under President William R. Harper, Professors Robert Francis Harper, Ira M. Price, George S. Goodspeed, Karl Budde, and James H. Breasted, and Drs. C. E. Crandall and G. R. Berry. To all my teachers I gratefully acknowledge my indebtedness, and especially to President William R. Harper and Professor Robert Francis Harper, under whose direction most of my work was done.

www.ingramcontent.com/pod-product-compliance
Lightning Source LLC
Chambersburg PA
CBHW020432010526
44118CB00010B/539